EARTH

Copyright © 2024 Samuel John

Hello! You are about to start an incredible journey to learn about our planet:

EARTH

You will discover that this wonderful place, which we call home, is full of fascinating things.

When and How Did Earth Form?

Earth formed about 4.6 billion years ago. But how?

It formed from rocks and dust that came together in space. Over time, it got so hot that it became a giant lava ball.

Then it cooled down and formed a solid surface where oceans and mountains appeared, and later, life emerged.

Earth is the third planet closest to the Sun in the Solar System.

It is one of the rocky planets because it is mainly made of rocks and minerals.

Earth looks like a blue ball from space because it is mostly covered with water.

If we could cut a small piece of Earth and look inside, we would see that it is made of three big layers:

- **Crust:** The outer layer, made of soil and rocks.
- **Mantle:** A thick layer under the crust, where rocks melt due to intense heat.
- **Core:** The center of the Earth, made mainly of metals like iron and nickel. It is extremely hot!

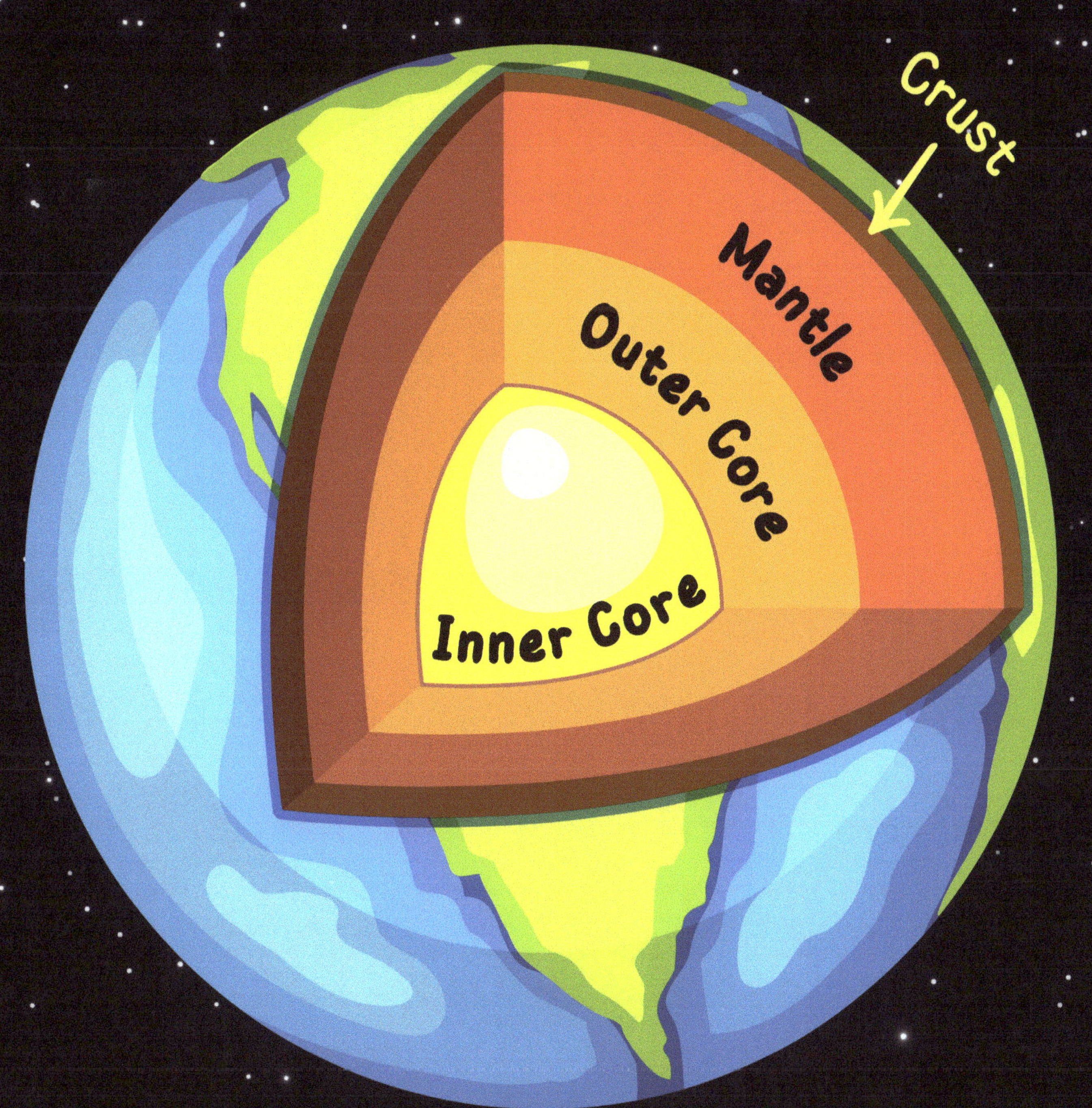

Crust
Mantle
Outer Core
Inner Core

How is Earth Structured?

Our planet has three major parts that make it habitable:

- **Geosphere:** All the rocks and lands, from the mountains to the bottom of the sea.
- **Hydrosphere:** All the water, covering 70% of the surface. This includes oceans, rivers, lakes, and even the frozen water at the poles.
- **Atmosphere:** A layer of gases that surrounds the whole planet. It protects us and makes life possible.

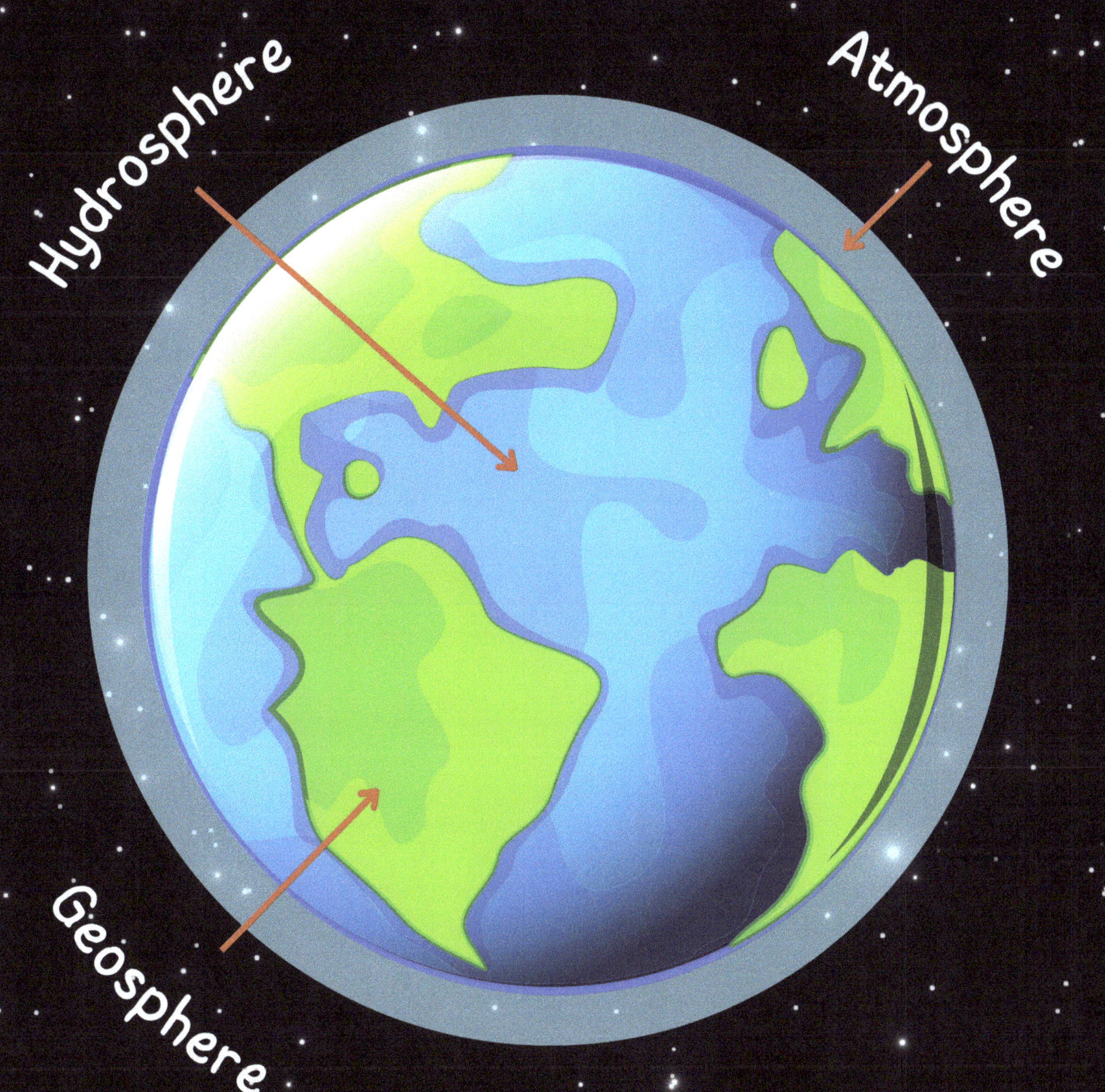

Hydrosphere
Atmosphere
Geosphere

- **Troposphere:** Where weather happens (rain, clouds, wind...) and where we live.
- **Stratosphere:** Where the ozone layer is that protects us from the Sun.
- **Mesosphere:** Where meteors burn up.
- **Thermosphere:** Where the Northern Lights happen.
- **Exosphere:** The outermost layer, where satellites and spacecraft orbit.

Exosphere
Thermosphere
Mesosphere
Stratosphere
Troposphere

As we saw earlier, the ozone layer is in the stratosphere.

It acts like a shield that protects us from the Sun's ultraviolet rays, which can cause health problems and damage marine and land ecosystems.

Earth's Rotation

Our planet has two important movements: rotation and revolution. Let's first look at rotation.

In this movement, Earth spins on its axis like a top.

It takes 24 hours to make a full turn, which is one day. This movement causes day and night. When one side of Earth faces the Sun, it is day. When it is on the opposite side, it is night.

In the revolution movement, Earth orbits around the Sun.

It takes 365 days to make a full orbit around the Sun, which is one year.

The revolution, along with the tilt of Earth's axis, causes the seasons: spring, summer, fall, and winter.

How is Life Possible on Earth?

Water: Earth has a lot of water, and water is essential for all living things.

Air: We have an atmosphere with air we can breathe. The oxygen in the air is crucial for plants, animals, and humans to survive.

Temperature: Earth's temperature is just right. It's not too hot or too cold, which allows plants to grow and animals to live comfortably.

Sun: The Sun provides us with the necessary light and heat. Plants use sunlight to nourish themselves through a process called photosynthesis.

Soil: Earth has fertile soil where plants can grow. Plants are important because they provide us with food and oxygen.

Protection: Earth has an ozone layer that protects us from harmful solar rays.

Taking Care of Our Planet

On April 22nd, we celebrate Earth Day to remember the importance of taking care of our home.

You can help protect planet Earth by recycling, saving water, using public transportation, and respecting all living things.

Earth is a wonderful place, and it is our duty to protect it. Every small gesture counts and helps us ensure a future for all living beings that call it home.

I hope you enjoyed learning about Earth. Take good care of our planet because it is the only home we have!

S	X	O	I	K	N	T	W	L	I	W	Z	J	J	Z
O	T	Y	X	J	J	J	Y	U	J	I	W	Q	S	P	N
O	Q	R	I	E	Q	N	G	G	S	L	L	V	P	E
B	N	Z	A	Z	D	N	X	E	X	L	D	Y	N	E
G	L	U	U	T	R	O	P	O	S	P	H	E	R	E
D	I	X	R	O	O	U	T	W	T	I	G	M	E	Y
O	J	Q	I	U	W	S	Q	P	C	Q	J	T	X	X
B	R	D	S	A	G	R	P	Q	S	H	G	K	O	Z
E	G	M	E	S	O	S	P	H	E	R	E	H	S	U
P	X	L	N	P	P	T	F	L	E	O	D	F	P	B
R	O	X	Q	T	B	S	A	H	A	R	U	H	H	V
B	J	T	H	E	R	M	O	S	P	H	E	R	E	X
V	S	J	H	H	B	L	H	J	L	C	K	N	R	O
R	N	L	R	P	S	M	I	L	F	P	T	H	E	X
Q	F	T	N	K	H	Q	W	T	X	T	Q	C	P	H

____

TROPOSPHERE   MESOSPHERE   EXOSPHERE

STRATOSPHERE   THERMOSPHERE

IDENTIFY
INNER CORE
OUTER CORE
MANTLE
CRUST

CROSSWORD

Across

[1] The part of the planet made up of rocks and land.
[4] Rays of the Sun from which the ozone layer protects us.
[5] Covers 70% of the earth's surface.
[6] Movement of the Earth when it spins on its axis.

Down

[2] Movement of the Earth around the Sun.
[3] The layer of the atmosphere where the ozone layer is.

IDENTIFY
GEOSPHERE   HYDROSPHERE
ATMOSPHERE

SOLUTIONS

Crust
Mantle
Outer Core
Inner Core

Hydrosphere
Atmosphere
Geosphere

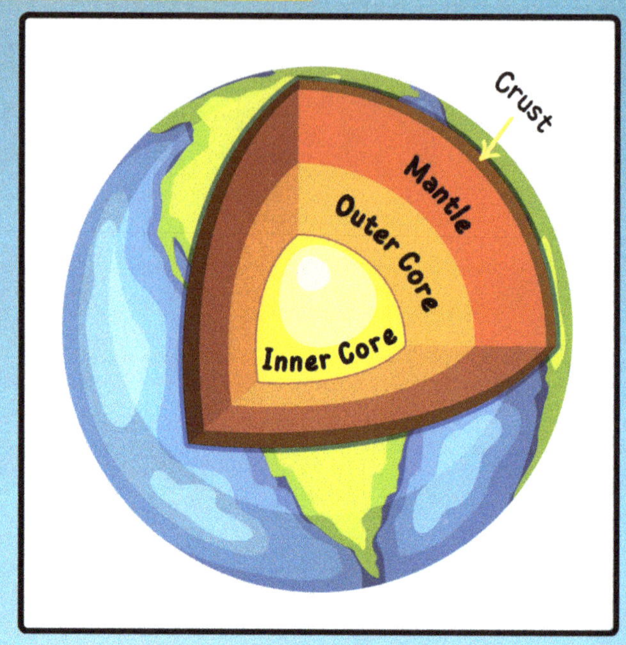

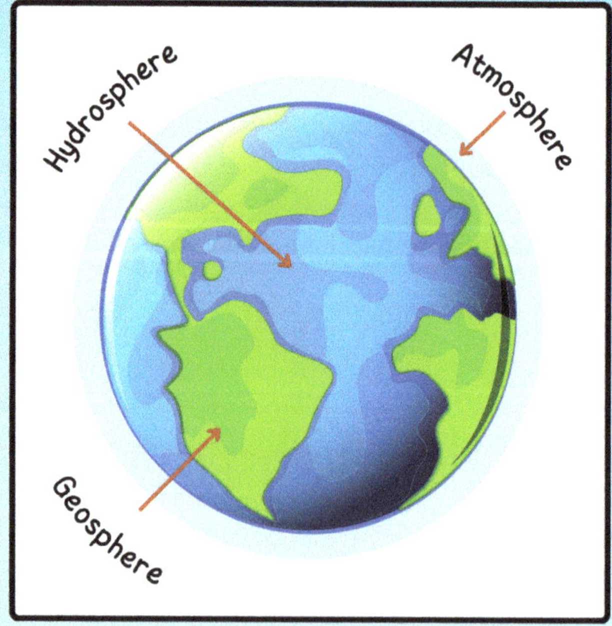

This book is the product of hard work, care, and dedication.

You might not know this, but I'm an independent author. Behind each of my books, there's only one person: me.

I handle every aspect of the process, from research to design... There's no big publishing house behind me, and I don't have illustrators. I take care of everything with a lot of love and enthusiasm. Whenever I publish a new book, it's almost like welcoming a new child into my life.

That's why I kindly ask you to consider all of this when leaving an honest review on the platform where you purchased this book. It would mean a lot to me, motivate me to keep going, and most importantly, provide valuable information for future readers.

I sincerely appreciate you taking a few seconds of your time to contribute your opinion to the world.

See you soon!

LEARN WITH OUR
EDUCATIONAL CHILDREN'S BOOKS

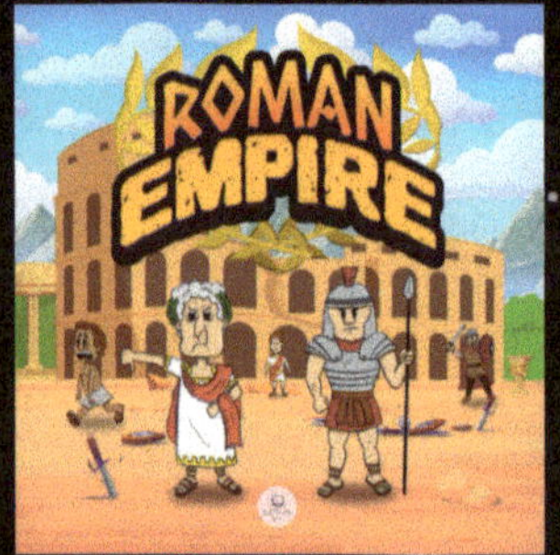

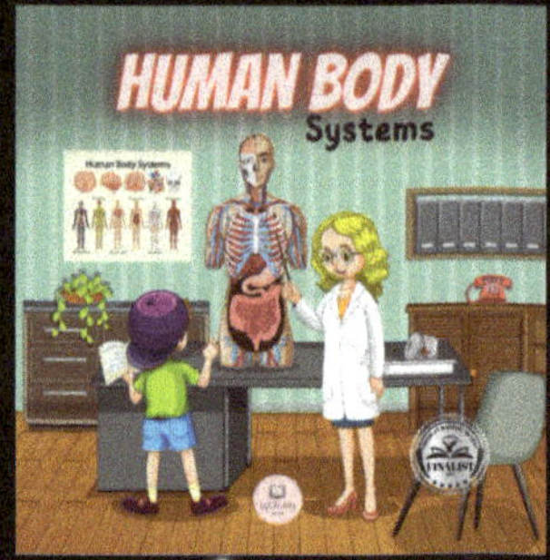

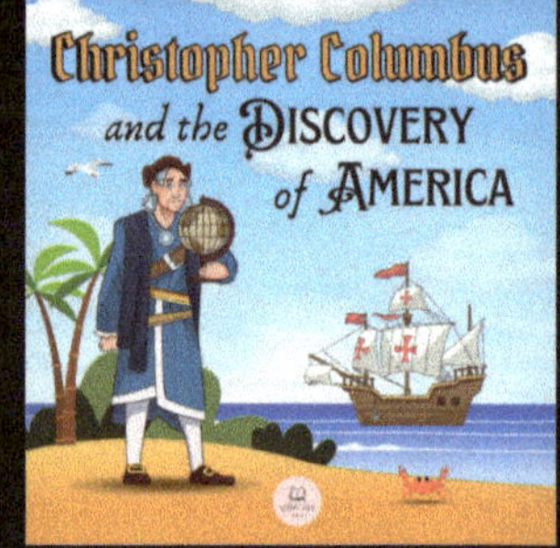

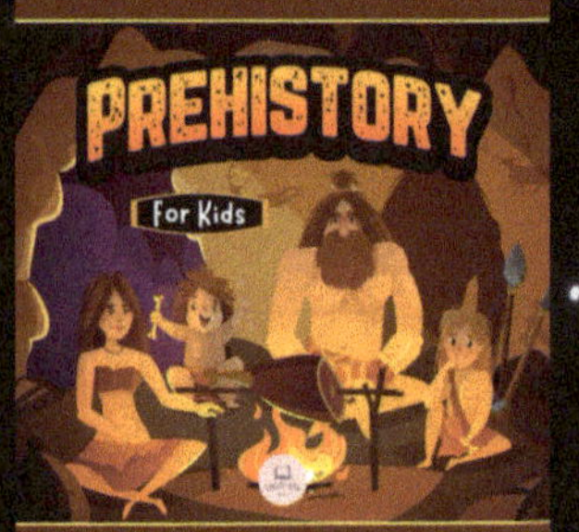

https://www.pge.me/childrensbooks

SAMMIE EXPLORES
THE SOLAR SYSTEM
Age 3-6

SCAN ME

SAMMIE EXPLORES
ANCIENT EGYPT

SCAN ME

HOW TO HANDLE
BULLYING

SCAN ME

The MOON
WHO PLAYED
HIDE AND SEEK

SCAN ME

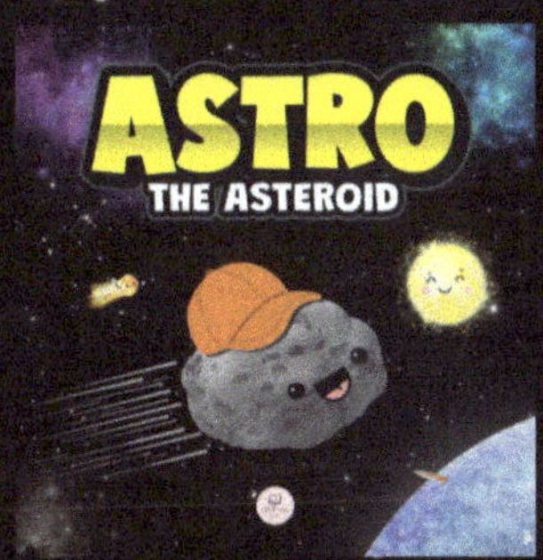

ASTRO
THE ASTEROID

SCAN ME

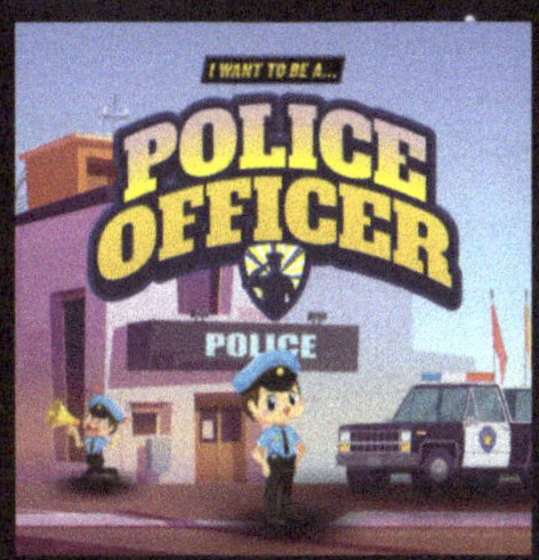

I WANT TO BE A...
POLICE OFFICER
POLICE

SCAN ME

The Steadfast
Tin Soldier

SCAN ME

SHARING IS CARING
with Shannon and Cam

SCAN ME

This book comes to life with downloadable audio. Perfect for engaging young readers and sparking their imagination.

www.ingramcontent.com/pod-product-compliance
Lightning Source LLC
LaVergne TN
LVHW070959180726
843512LV00017B/1270